Contents

Peacocks or peanuts –
Dr Dean looks at strange phobias

Dr Dean

If you have a phobia, it means that you are very frightened of something. I don't mean something boring, like a maths test, or getting a spot on your chin … or even a trip to the dentist.

Some phobias seem very strange – from fish to buttons, teapots, fleas, clouds, bees, peaches and cream cakes – all of them have been reasons for phobias.

WELCOME TO WIGAN

You may get panic attacks when you have to face the subject of your phobia.
This means that:

- your heart beats very fast
- you can't breathe easily
- you feel sick
- your mouth feels dry.

And phobias can get in the way – if you are frightened of travelling by plane, you may be spending all your holidays in sunny Wigan!

Some phobias:

Jin

"I am frightened of spiders – such hairy legs!

I can't take a spider out of the bath.

I can't look at a photo of a spider –

I can't even think about spiders!"

Roy

"I have a phobia about peanut butter.

As soon as I see that jar, I start to feel sick.

When I was little, my dad made me eat

10 peanut butter sandwiches

and I think that started the phobia."

Jane

"I hate the number 13.

I have lots of bad dreams about it.

I will be 13 soon,

and I can't face the birthday cards.

Lots of number 13s on the windowsill!"

Bea

"I'm frightened of the sea!

If I go to the beach,

I panic and I have to leave.

My mates think it's funny –

they can be really mean!"

Jack

"I panic if I see a peacock.

I start to shake and my knees feel weak.

But I can't let it defeat me.

And – lucky for me – there aren't

many peacocks in Leeds."

Dean

"Baked beans!

I'm really frightened of them.

If I see baked beans on my plate,

I can't eat the meal and I want to scream.

My mates all tease me about it."

Phobias can be hard to deal with but you will be pleased to know that help is at hand.

Let's take the case of Jin – the boy who freaks out if he sees a spider. He can be shown a way to face spiders in small steps:

Step 1

Jin looks at a photo of a spider (not a man-eating tarantula – just a bog-standard bathroom job).

Step 2

Now things start to get real.
Poor old Jin has to look at a live spider – but it's in a glass tank, so he will feel safe.

Step 3

Ta-da!
The lid is taken off the tank, and now Jin has to put his hand in – and touch the spider!
If he can do this last step, he has got over his phobia.

**Have you got a phobia? Has anyone you know got one?
Phobias are more common than you may think!**

Monsters
of land, air and sea

In Greek legends, you can read about lots of amazing beasts. Here are some of the meanest ...

The Sirens

The Sirens were sweet-looking females who, seated on the beach, tempted seamen from their ships with enchanting songs. When they reached the shore, the men went to sleep and were eaten by the Sirens. Odysseus had to be bound to the mast of his ship to avoid the Sirens' song, as he longed to go to them.

The Cyclops

The Cyclops was a massive beast with just one round eye. He made lightning bolts for the king of the Greek gods, Zeus. He imprisoned Odysseus and his men in a cave, but they escaped. They hid in the fleeces of sheep!

Scylla

This deep-sea demon gave Odysseus a big problem!

Scylla was a female monster with 6 faces, 18 rows of teeth and 12 legs. She didn't speak, but she had a high-pitched scream. She lived in a cave and snatched seamen from their ships.

Odysseus had a narrow escape from Scylla. The monster left him weak, but he managed to retreat – at top speed!

Free at last.

The Minotaur

A mean monster, the Minotaur had a man's body but the neck, face and horns of a bull. He lived in a maze, and each decade, 7 boys and 7 girls were sent into the maze for him to eat.

The Harpies

Harpies were girls with wings (or birds with no beaks and girls' faces).

These fantastic females enjoyed unleashing storms and whirlwinds.

In the tale of *Jason and the Golden Fleece*, a man offended the gods, so the Harpies grabbed his meals, leaving just scraps.

Satyrs

Part-man and part-beast, the horned Satyrs dressed in animal skins and wreaths of green leaves and grapes. They enjoyed sleeping, eating and dancing.

The Gorgons

The Gorgons were three sisters. They had wings, and their hair was made from coiled snakes. Each Gorgon had glaring eyes, a big mouth and large, pointed tusks.

The Sphinx

This female beast had the face of a girl, the wings of a bird and the body of a big cat. She guarded the entrance to the Greek city of Thebes and all visitors had to solve a problem before they went in.

It was this: 'Which animal goes on 4 feet first, then on 2 feet, and then on 3 feet?' Can you guess? (See bottom of page.)

Only Oedipus got it right. The Sphinx was so displeased she jumped off her high rock and that was the end of her!

Man – he goes on 4 feet as a baby, on 2 feet as an adult and then on 2 feet plus 1 (a walking stick) as an old man

Down the hatch!

Sometimes I think I'm the only boy in our street that eats normal stuff. Pies, spuds, the odd green thing if I have to. (Five a day? More like five a lifetime with me!) But not all boys and girls are like me. Ted next door turns a shade of bright green if he so much as smells a carrot! Kate at number nine lives on nothing but pasta, mushrooms and marmite, and Eric three doors down claims he's never even seen rice, let alone scoffed it – and he's nineteen!

I invited kids to send me horrid tales of frightful foods. These are the nice ones (the rest are too horrid to print!) ...

"The lights went out in our house one night when we were eating dinner. In the dark, I picked up what I took to be a ripe tomato and popped it in my mouth. It slipped down right away. It turned out I'd picked up my gran's glass eye by mistake. Oops! I was sick for nine days."

(Tom, 11, from Glasgow)

"My dad tells us that when he was a boy, his family was so poor that they had to set traps to catch mice for supper. He says they tasted nice, fried with a slice of lime. He ate a crocodile too. Really! My mum says it's bad to tell lies to kids, but he just smiles and winks at me. Is he pulling my leg?"

(Sally, 9, from Bristol)

"My brother's mate, Josh, is a right fool. He eats peanut butter and jam sandwiches. That's fine, you may think. But if you give him *anything* to put in it, he eats that too. One day, outside our house, I picked up a slug from the path, full of slime and goo. Into the butty it went, and gulp! He let it slide down inside his belly – disgusting! It was so funny, I nearly cried, but my mum went mad. She made Josh go home, and I'm grounded for a week."

(Jack, 12, from Preston)

"My grandad eats tripe. It's white, it looks like rubber, and it's from the insides of a sheep's tummy. And that's no lie!"

(Lorna, 8, from Cardiff)

"My mate says there's a man and his wife that live in the woods near him. At night, he checks the roads to collect animals that have been run over. Magpies, rabbits, hedgehogs, the lot. He scrapes them up, then his wife roasts them on a campfire. You can hear the burps for miles around."

(Jie, 13, from Bristol)

"Last week, my pal Barry ate my watch. He's always on time for lessons now. That's the good bit. But if it's really silent at reading time, you can hear him ticking at the back of the room. That's spooky."

(Ben, 11, from Bradford)

"I don't know if this is true, but my mate Mike says there's a boy in his class that eats woodlice! No kidding! He mixes them up with rice, sticks them in the freezer and eats them like lollipops. Ice 'n' rice 'n' lice. Not nice!"

(Alex, 9, from Nottingham)

Wild Mike's
guide to staying alive!

Hi kids! I'm Wild Mike and I'm here to keep you alive!

Stop! Before you turn the page and rush on to the next text, I must tell you that most animals will never dream of attacking a human. They will only attack if they get a sudden fright or shock, or if they think you will harm them or their family.

But ... there are beasts out there that will not only attack humans, but will have them for lunch afterwards. Eek!

So here's Wild Mike's advice on what to avoid if you'd like to stay alive and kicking.

If you come across a **big cat** that's not in a zoo, the chances are it's going to be bad news. They're big, fast, have razor-sharp claws, and they like to eat meat ... lots of it. If you see a lion, tiger or leopard, best get on your bike – fast!

The Lions of Tsavo

Over nine months in 1898, two lions killed and ate at least 35 bridge workers in Tsavo, Kenya. They crept into the camp at night and dragged the men out of their tents.

Bears normally stay away from humans, but if they run out of fish and small animals to eat, you need to watch out. They might just fancy a nice, plump, ripe hiker! Grizzly bears can run fast, they can climb trees, swim in rivers, and they are big!

But what about those cuddly white polar bears, you may ask. Take Mike's advice: if you spot one out there on the ice, run for your life – it's a killer too.

Fancy a swim in the sea? Nice idea, but keep an eye out for that tell-tale fin. **Sharks** have lines of teeth like spikes. They will slice you up in no time!

Hmm, maybe a swim in the river then? Fine, but not in the River Nile. Don't be fooled by the smile of the **crocodile** as it opens its jaws wide. It will slide into the water, glide towards you unseen, then snap! You're a human takeaway, looking at life from inside a croc's fat belly!

Believe it or not!

Today, you can pay money to be eaten by fish. In some clinics, you can stick your tired feet in a tank of water while a hundred tiny fish bite off the dead skin. Nice or not? You decide.

It's also not wise to lie down for a nap after your swim. You may wake up (or maybe not!) to find yourself an ant's lunch. African **army ants** hunt in gangs of thousands, and their knife-like teeth will munch up everything in their path – including you.

Yikes!

And if the ants don't get you, the snakes might. **Pythons** can grow up to nine metres, and will squeeze the life out of you. There are lots of reports of pythons eating humans, but not much proof, so you may be OK.

But then again ...

Help!

The phone zone

Mobile phones – most of us don't know life without them, but there was a time when all phones had to be attached to a phone socket.

If you were out with your mates and needed to phone home, you had to go to a public phone box, put coins in a slot, and then speak quickly before your time ran out!

You could put more cash in, but you had to have the right coins. Phone boxes are still around, but the Post Office (they own the phone boxes in the UK) say they will slowly get rid of them as more of us have our own mobile phones.

Do you know what "mobile" means? It means "easily moved about". So that fancy camera phone of yours is an "easily moved about phone" – catchy, eh? What about the word "phone"? That is short for "telephone" – and that is from the Greek for "far" (tele) and for "sound" (phone). Telephone – far away sound!

Those of us who like gadgets enjoy checking out the latest games and gizmos on the most up-to-date phones, but some grown-ups are what we call "technophobes"! They have a phobia (fear of) technology. I bet you can think of an adult who panics in the mobile phone zone. Yes? Then enjoy Shane's tale of his technophobe dad ...

Hello! I'm Shane and I have a bone to pick with adults and mobile phones.

They think they know what to do with them, but they don't.

They get a cool phone, press all the buttons, say the jargon – and then get in a mess.

When they can't cope, they ask us to sort it!

Sound like your mum? Dad? Gran? Does it drive you mad?

Read on – you are not alone!

Dad:	Hmm ... got a really good phone. It has blue teeth.
Shane:	I think you mean tooth, Dad.
Dad:	That's what I said.
Shane:	Do you know what Bluetooth is for?
Dad:	Er ... yeess ... it's why I chose this phone. I needed blue ... thingy.
Shane:	Tooth. Bluetooth. It means you connect in an instant to lots of phones at the same time. You can send pics, videos and stuff like that to all your mates. Bluetooth connectivity, Dad. Radio waves.
Dad:	Duh! I know that!

Shane: Have you put your PIN in then?

Dad: I had a go. Kept getting it wrong.
Three times I did it, but it won't switch on.

Shane: Uh oh – get the code wrong three times and it goes into "blocked code mode".

Dad: Sounds bad. What do I have to do to make it go into "unblocked code mode" then?

Shane: You need the PUK code, Dad.

Dad: PUK?

Shane: Personal Unlocking Key.
I'll sort it. You get me a can of pop. Make yourself a cup of tea.

A while later ...

Umm ...

Shane: Have you set your profiles yet?

Dad: My what?

Shane: Your profiles. Let's start with a ringtone. Just look at this list till you find one you like.

Dad: These are ringtones?

Shane: That's right.

Dad: Really? 'Snowflakes'? 'Peppermint'? 'Time Travel'? I was hoping for a nice bit of classical music. Something soothing.

Shane: I don't think you'll get anything like that, Dad. But if not, you can always get it from the App Store.

Dad: But I haven't got time to go to the shops now – I have to sort this phone out. And your mother's got the car.

Shane: Oh, Dad! The App Store's an online shop. You pay for the ringtone from your phone.

Dad: Oh. Well, yes, yes. I, um, know that. But where …?

Shane: What's the problem now?

Dad: Where do you put the money in? There's no slot for the coins. Didn't they think about that when they made the phone?

Shane: Dad, you put your bank details in, then you pay for things online from the App Store.

Dad: Bank details … right. OK, I'll do it in the morning.

Shane: But why do it in the morning? Why not now?

Dad: Because it's past 6 o'clock. The App Store will be closed now.

Shane: It's hopeless. I give up!

Home-grown sound effect zone!

The harsh tone of an evil Dalek has sent lots of children into the 'behind the sofa' zone, but imagine a *Doctor Who* episode without sound effects. I don't suppose an exploding Dalek or Cyberman would be very exciting with just a puff of silent smoke, would it? All those zaps, clangs, booms and bangs are what bring it all to life.

Every episode of a TV drama or a film script will have short notes called sound effect lines. From everyday sounds such as:

man blows his nose

or

mobile phone rings

to those more dramatic events such as:

caravan explodes

or

lorry blows up.

Even your school play needs sound effects, and everyday objects give you lots of scope to make your own! Check out this home-grown sound effect zone!

🔊 Staging a fight? Drop big books for lifelike punches and thumps.

🔊 For the sound of a small bird trapped in an enclosed space, try flapping a pair of leather gloves about.

🔊 Suppose you need a broken bone or two? Snap crisp, fresh celery sticks in half. So convincing it hurts!

🔊 If the need ever arose for the sound of a bat flapping its wings (you never know), open and close an umbrella at great speed. Close it more slowly for a big bird (*an eagle flying low and slow*).

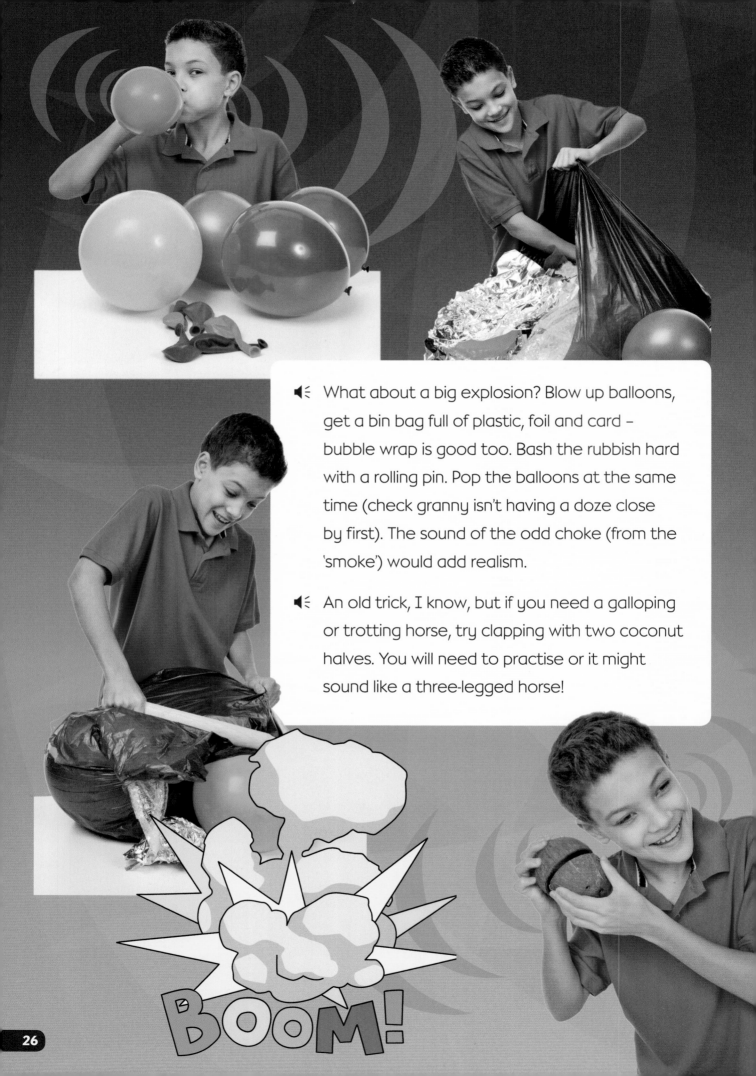

🔊 What about a big explosion? Blow up balloons, get a bin bag full of plastic, foil and card – bubble wrap is good too. Bash the rubbish hard with a rolling pin. Pop the balloons at the same time (check granny isn't having a doze close by first). The sound of the odd choke (from the 'smoke') would add realism.

🔊 An old trick, I know, but if you need a galloping or trotting horse, try clapping with two coconut halves. You will need to practise or it might sound like a three-legged horse!

BOOM!

Compose your own!

Have a go at adding sound effects where this silly script asks for them. Those marked with ⚡ are explained in the home-grown sound effect zone. There are also some that you will have to work out how to make yourself. Give it a go!

Scene 1:

⚡ *Sound of horse's hooves.*

Prince No Hope: I rode all night to win the hand of the princess!

⚡ *Small bird in cage flaps its wings.*

Prince No Hope: I have this bird as a gift (actually I stole it as I am flat broke).

He knocks.

Servant: Another poser wanting the princess.

Sound of keys rattling.
Door creaks open.

Scene 2:

Princess Cyclone: Yet another prince who thinks I want him to propose to me! I like living on my own (with a servant or two, no, make that three). I'll give that prince a dose of my Kung Fu moves – that'll show him.

⚡ *A scream followed by punches.*

Scene 3:

Prince No Hope: Goodness! She can keep her throne!

⚡ *Jumps on horse and gallops off home.*

Duke weds royal bride in wedding of the season!

A worldwide exclusive from our royal correspondent, June Bluestocking.

On a fine Tuesday in June, it was all smiles as handsome Duke Tam Lin and Princess Janet tied the knot. The pair met and found true love in the forest, where the Princess is in the habit of wafting about, picking bluebells.

The blushing bride was given away by her proud father the King, ruler of all Fairyland, and she was attended by three imps. She wore a dress made of rare dragonfly wings, set off by the sparkly gold fairy dust in her hair (she may be a royal princess, but she has her girly moments!) She held a bunch of her trademark bluebells.

The groom, a duke with a huge fortune, enjoys fighting duels and killing dragons in his free time. His best man was his brother, Sir Luke, who, sadly, has been changed into a frog. (He had to stand on a pillar to do the bit with the rings.) And there was more scandal when his fairy steed, a mule called Jules, disgraced itself at an important point in the speeches.

VIP guests included proud mother-of-the-bride Queen Jude, who wore a blue hat with fluffy pink and green plumes. She is divorced from the King, and at first refused to speak to him – in fact, she tipped some fairy fizz over him! But they made a truce for this important day.

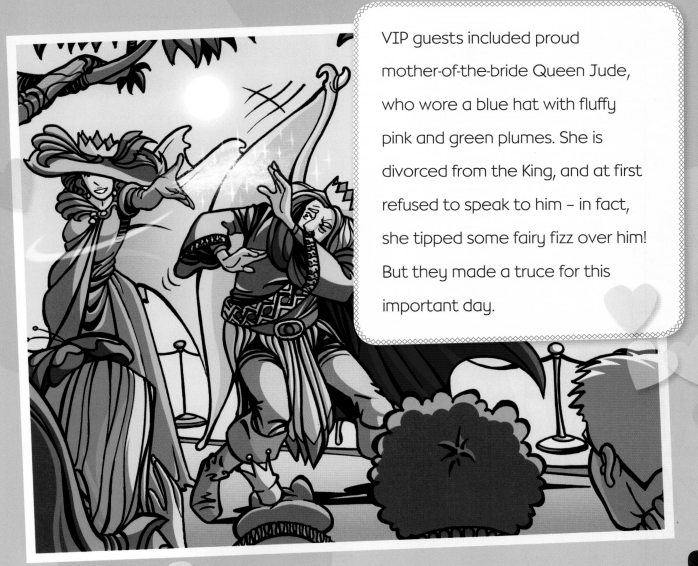

The wedding bash was held at the royal palace. Glam guests dined on fairy cakes and chilled lemonade (produced by a great team of water nymphs), and lifted their glasses to wish the bride and groom "good elf". They then danced under the moon (music by a band of forest fairy flute players – how classy is that?) At midnight, they gave Tam and Janet a real royal send-off on their honeymoon in Never Never Land.

The happy event was almost spoiled by a handful of gate-crashers – goblins and gremlins – who had a fight with the groom's family and then refused to leave. In the end, they were driven away by the water nymphs, who proved to be quite strong!

Wedding presents included a lute, six teapots and a palace!

Tam and Janet's huge palace has ten thousand bedrooms (princesses in fairy tales can have that sort of thing), and they will both drive swanky gold carriages pulled by milk-white steeds.

What they said:

Princess Janet: *(sigh)* I really, really ♥ him! Have you seen his cute dukey smile? And he's got brilliant contacts in the dragon-slaying business! What more could a girl ask for?? *(More sighs and blushes)*

Duke Tam Lin: At last, I've found the girl of my dreams! Only thing is – she hates it when I go off to fight duels with the lads. But I'd much rather stay in and watch TV with my sweet wife!

Sir Luke: The gate-crashers were hard brutes. A small frog like me was no match for them. Very handy with their fists, don't you know?

Queen Jude: Are you taking a photo of me? Will it be in one of those posh celeb mags? Ooh, let me put more lippy on! What was I saying? Well, our Janet used to go out with a banshee called Bruce. I wasn't all that keen on him – he never stopped screeching. Tam is a much better catch – such a nice boy! But that rude mule! Fancy doing that on the carpet – with the groom's speech in progress, too!

The wedding webcam can be seen on the royal website www.kingoffairyland@palace.celebs.uk.

Happy ever after?

Can you spot a chance for a bit of fairy tale magic? Do this quick quiz to find out if a 'happy ever after' ending is going to happen for you!

1. **A huge frog blocks your path and refuses to hop it. Do you:**

a. Make Mummy scoop it up and put it in the *huge* pond in your *huge* garden, where it can live happily ever after with all its mates.

b. Scream. You have a frog phobia. Consumed with panic, you go a bit green yourself and pass out (this is not the coolest choice).

c. Give the big, green thing a kiss just in case, by a fluke, it transforms into a true blue prince or princess.

2. Walking in some woods, you spot a tall tower. You see long, golden tresses flowing out of the highest window and tumbling to the ground. Do you:

a. Carry on walking. It may look like a climbing rope, but Mummy says there is no excuse for climbing things.

b. Feel a bit confused. Why would a girl throw her hair out of a window? Is it a trick? You can't climb up there anyway. You get dizzy just going up a flight of stairs!

c. You think there must be a golden-haired girl trapped up there! You don't think the owner of the golden locks will be amused when you use them as a climbing rope, but you must rescue her!

3. Everyone but you is asked to a fancy dress party. It's so unfair it makes you fume. Do you:

a. Invite yourself! They must have just forgotten to tell you. You don't need to spend a fortune on a costume. You use a pair of Mummy's woolly tights and your great-great-great grand-daddy's plumed hat (he was a duke, of course), and you go as the Grand Old Duke of York.

b. Put on your music for a groovy tune or two, stick pineapple chunks and cheese on cocktail sticks and party until you are blue in the face. All alone. Dressed as a chicken. Sad, but true.

c. Sit in your room but assume that a good fairy will sort out a costume, transport, and someone with a fortune who will ask to marry you.

4. **You find a dusty, unused mirror in the attic. Do you:**

a. Amuse yourself posing and insist it is put in your bedroom with the other 15. Then check with Mummy that you are still the best-looking child in the land.

b. Think you could do with a bit of grooming. You just have to squeeze it through the attic hatch and heave it down the steps. Don't drop … oh – too late! That's 2555 days of bad luck, I assume?

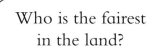

Who is the fairest in the land?

c. Talk to it. Yes – that's right, you talk to it. You ask if your fab haircut looks cool, and you assume it will talk back! Ask it, 'Who is the fairest in the land?' and it will say, 'You are' (unless you're not, of course!).

Scores

Mostly As: You may have a fairy tale life, but remember what happened to the Selfish Giant? Be a bit less rude and spoiled for a true happy ending!

Mostly Bs: Your life is more scary tale than fairy tale, but keep trying and one day your fortunes will change!

Mostly Cs: You are always up for a bit of magic! Happy ever after endings rule for you!

The End!

Awesome!

Lots of kids want to be pop stars. But what about you?

🎧 Have you caught the pop star bug?

🎧 Would you do anything for an audience?

🎧 Are you dreaming of your first gig?

🎧 Are you hungry for applause?

🎧 HAVE YOU GOT ... THE TALENT FACTOR?

If you said, "yes, yes, yes, yes and yes" ... read on!

Thousands of kids and teenagers enter contests like "The X Factor" and "The Voice" – in the UK and in America. And yes, most of them are disappointed, because there can only be one winner. It's a hard thing to do – after all, could you take the comments Simon dishes out? Enter at your own risk!

You can have just as much fun in the school band, or with your mates. Check out different sorts of music – pop, rock, jazz, hip-hop, rhythm and blues ...

If you can sing – fantastic! But if you have an awful voice (if you sound like a macaw with beak-ache), you can still be in a band. Think electric guitars and drum kits – or mouth organs and electric pianos! Saxophones are really cool, too. There are lots of instruments to choose from, and you can be taught to play any of them. Don't forget – you will also need an amp and speakers, if you really want to make some noise!

All the best bands have one thing in common – they practise, practise, practise! So if *you* want that top billing, you know what you have to do! And yes, you will have to get earplugs for the rest of the family!

Paul Dawson (16): I've been in the Jackdaws since I was 13. I play the drums, but if I try to sing, I bawl like a banshee! It makes your skin crawl! It's not my fault, but the lead singer tells me to stick to the drums!

Dawn Morgan (17): No one in my family is in the music business. I'm the daughter of a roofer and a school cook. But all the kids tell me I've got an awesome voice, with a real American drawl!

If you want to be a pro in the music business, you don't have to sing or play an instrument. You can be a:

graphic designer
(designing artwork
and posters)

songwriter

dancer

stylist
(hair and clothes)

manager

DJ
(in a club or
on the radio)

reporter

sound engineer

photographer

lighting engineer

recording engineer

If you don't fancy any of these jobs, don't just yawn and give up! Get a job in your local music store. You can listen to all the best bands, and they will pay you to do it – as long as you do some work as well!

The Fab Factor

Kermit O'Bleary: Good evening, and welcome to the show. I'd like to introduce our panel, Louis Squelch, Simon Towel, and the delightful Nicole Smerzy!

Applause from the audience.

Kermit: Let's say a big hello to our first act – Daddy Cool!

Daddy Cool saunters on to the stage.

Simon: And your job is?

Daddy Cool: *(In an American drawl)*

I'm a club DJ.

That's what I say.
I mix tracks,
I chillax...

Simon:	*(Yawning)* OK, pal. Can you sing?
Daddy Cool:	Um – no, bro.
Simon:	Can you play?
Daddy Cool:	No, bro.
Simon:	What can you do, Daddy?
Daddy Cool:	I can rap! Bring on the bling! I got a big, gold ring And a necklace sort of thing! Ding-a-ling, ding-a-ling. I can rap to hip-hop! I don't want to stop …
Simon:	Stop! You call that rap? You want us to clap? And as for that cap … You foolish chap! I don't like your chances, pal. You should be banned! It's a big no from me. Louis?

Louis:	*(With a huge guffaw)* No. Nicole?
Nicole:	No, Daddy Cool. Sorry! Big kiss! *(Blows Daddy Cool a kiss)*

Audience boos Daddy Cool off.

Kermit:	Let's have a big hand for the next act – a fab girl band!

Applause from the audience as 3 girls prance on to the stage.

Laura:	I'm Laura, this is Paula and this is Maureen. We are the Daughters of Darkness! We have raw talent. We have the full-on Fab Factor! We sing indie rock! *(Well, me and Paula do.)*
Nicole:	Ooh! Saucer of milk for Laura, please! Draw your claws in, madam!
Louis:	Show us what you can do, girls.
Daughters of Darkness:	*(Screeching)* Ooooooh-hoooooo, oooooooh-hooooo …

Simon:	What an awful tune! Who taught you to bawl like that? I want you to withdraw from the show! Hold the applause!
Laura:	It's all your fault, Maureen!

The Daughters of Darkness exit.

Kermit:	Let me introduce – um – Mr Saunders.

To applause from the audience, Mr Saunders limps on to the stage. He looks about 100.

Mr Saunders:	*(In a thin, high-pitched voice)* I'm going to sing an Elvis song …
Louis:	*(In a taunting voice)* Best of luck with that, pal!
Simon:	Tut tut! Sit on the naughty step, Louis!

Nicole:	*(Soothingly, to Mr Saunders)* Bring it on, babe!
Mr Saunders:	*(Starts to sing)* Way – hay – I'm all shook up …
Simon:	No! Stop! You're awful! Get off!
Mr Saunders:	Eh? What did you say?
Simon:	Get off! Get off!
Mr Saunders:	Eh? Eh? What's that you say?

Simon stands up, with a deep sigh.

Simon:	This is the last straw! Send for my private jet! I'm off to my 40 room pad in LA!
Kermit:	Simon Towel has left the building. See you next week, boys and girls.

Peacocks or peanuts – Dr Dean looks at strange phobias (ea)

Green words: *Say the sounds. Say the word.*

weak   real   mean   fleas   cream   beats   breathe   scream   meal   deal

Say the syllables. Say the word.

tea|pots   pea|cock   rea|sons   eas|i|ly   thir|teen

Say the root word. Say the whole word.

peach → peaches   fright → frighten → frightened

Red words: anyone who something they want small

Challenge words: phobia touch heart like over dry spider very even number butter photo live tarantula now

Vocabulary check: **phobia** *an extreme fear*   **bog-standard** *something ordinary or common*

Monsters of land, air and sea (ea)

Green words: *Say the sounds. Say the word.*

sea   read   beasts   beach   speak   scream   weak   mean   each

beaks   meals   wreaths   leaves

Say the syllables. Say the word.

re|treat   un|leash|ing   dis|pleased

Say the root word. Say the whole word.

mean → meanest   seat → seated   reach → reached   leave → leaving

sleep → sleeping   eat → eaten → eating

Red words: were who their they was one some here

Challenge words: monster Sirens Odysseus Cyclops eye Zeus Scylla Minotaur Satyrs Sphinx guarded Thebes guess Oedipus females demon Golden glaring baby old

Vocabulary check: **enchanting** *charming, magical*   **imprisoned** *kept in prison, captive*

retreat *withdraw, run away*   **bound** *tied*

Down the hatch! (i–e ie)

Green words: *Say the sounds. Say the word.*

five   like   nine   rice   time   nice   ripe   mice   lime   smiles   lice

lie   slime   tripe   white   miles

Say the syllables. Say the word.

mag|pie   croc|o|dile   out|side   si|lent

Say the root word. Say the whole word.

cry → cried   slip → slipped

Red words: sometimes   all   one   were   they   brother   there   watch

Challenge words: tomato   eye   only   campfire   turns   down
claims   even   alone   these   nearly   hear   burps   now   true

Vocabulary check: gulp *swallow*

Wild Mike's guide to staying alive! (i–e ie)

Green words: *Say the sounds. Say the word.*

Mike   bike   nine   ripe   white   ice   life   lines   spikes   slice   time

Nile   smile   wide   slide   glide   while   bite   wise   lie   knife   yikes

Say the syllables. Say the word.

a|live   ad|vice   cro|co|dile   de|cide

Red words: here   they   their   there   what   come   watch   one

water   some

Challenge words: human   only   afterwards   news   tiger   leopard
Tsavo   months   workers   bears   eye   everything   including
metres   wild   guide   turn   most   they're   claws   lion   climb
those   idea   opens   jaws   believe   money   dead   python

Vocabulary check: avoid *keep away from*   **glide** *smooth, quiet motion*

The phone zone (o–e)

Green words: *Say the sounds. Say the word.*

phone   zone   cope   mode   code   bone   home

Say the syllables. Say the word.

tech|no|phobe   tel|e|phone   a|lone   ring|tone   hope|less

Say the root word. Say the whole word.

slow ➔ slowly   hope ➔ hoping

Red words: who   there   all   were   could   some   call   mother   where

Challenge words: down   mobile   most   post   word   fear   blue   why   videos
won't   key   profiles   music   now   money   details

Vocabulary check: bone to pick with adults *a bit annoyed about something that adults do*
gizmo *a gadget, bit of technology*   **jargon** *technical language*

Home-grown sound effect zone! (o–e)

Green words: *Say the sounds. Say the word.*

home   zone   smoke   notes   nose   scope   bone   close   choke
Hope   rode   broke   dose

Say the syllables. Say the word.

ep|i|sode   supp|ose   a|rose   prop|ose

Say the root word. Say the whole word.
broke ➔ broken   enclose ➔ enclosed   slow ➔ slowly   pose ➔ poser

Red words: would   called   where   there   want   who   all   two
great   small   another

Challenge words: Cyberman   every   even   celery   half   hurts   leather
gloves   explosion   halves   work   scene   Cyclone   Kung Fu
moves   her   Dalek   behind   sofa   keys   explained

Vocabulary check: convincing *realistic, life-like*   **propose** *make an offer of marriage*
scope *opportunity*

Duke weds royal bride in wedding of the season! (u–e ue)

Green words: *Say the sounds. Say the word.*

duke   June   true   rude   duels   Luke   mule   brutes   Jules   truce

Say the syllables. Say the word.

blue|bells   Tues|day   for|tune

Say the root word. Say the whole word.

refuse → refused   include → included   use → used   duke → dukey

Red words: love   water   watch   brother   mother   father   their
could   all   where   great   who   were   there   small   some   one

Challenge words: worldwide   dragonfly   guests   nymphs   business   how
her   carriages   rather   music   exclusive   over   very   wafting   ruler   rare
moments   almost   proved   both   only   photo

Vocabulary check: banshee *a spirit that screams and wails*   **mule** *an old horse*
swanky *expensive, flashy and posh*   **truce** *temporarily stop fighting*   **scandal** *something disgraceful*

Happy ever after? (u–e ue)

Green words: *Say the sounds. Say the word.*

huge   fluke   true   blue   use   fume   duke   tune   rude   rule

Say the syllables. Say the word.

ex|cuse   res|cue   for|tune   cos|tume   a|ssume   pre|sume

Say the root word. Say the whole word.

refuse → refuses   consume → consumed   cool → coolest   confuse → confused
amuse → amused   plume → plumed   groom → grooming

Red words: where   walking   some   there   they   who   tall   other
through   talk   one   could   would   two   everyone   great

Challenge words: ever   after   phobia   tower   golden   course   down
remember   scary   climbing   why   old   trying

Vocabulary check: phobia *an extreme fear*   **plumed** *decorated with feathers*
fluke *by strange chance*   **true blue** *top quality, the real thing*   **consumed** *eaten up*

Awesome! (aw au)

Green words: *Say the sounds. Say the word.*

y<u>aw</u>n   cr<u>aw</u>l   D<u>aw</u>n   P<u>au</u>l

Say the syllables. Say the word.

<u>au</u>|di|en<u>ce</u>   ma|c<u>aw</u>   D<u>aw</u>|son   be|c<u>au</u>se   app|l<u>au</u>se   <u>aw</u>|ful

Say the root word. Say the whole word.

rec<u>or</u>d → rec<u>or</u>ding   rep<u>or</u>t → rep<u>or</u>ter

---

Red words: <u>th</u>ere   <u>th</u>ey   s<u>ai</u>d   want   <u>wh</u>at   w<u>o</u>uld   any   <u>one</u>   <u>all</u>   c<u>ou</u>ld   s<u>ome</u>

Challenge words: busine<u>ss</u>   music   t<u>ee</u>nagers   pianos   <u>a</u>che   g<u>ui</u>tars   radio   manag<u>er</u>   danc<u>er</u>   c<u>augh</u>t   t<u>augh</u>t   <u>awe</u>some   th<u>e͡se</u>   w<u>or</u>k   most   only   <u>ear</u>plugs   try   d<u>augh</u>ter   pro   song|writer   stylist   engin<u>eer</u>   desi<u>gn</u>er   post<u>er</u>s   Simon   rh<u>y</u>thm   sp<u>ea</u>kers   <u>ph</u>otogra<u>ph</u>er   rep<u>or</u>ter

---

Vocabulary check: **banshee** *a spirit that screams and wails*   **bawl** *shout loudly*
drawl *to speak with drawn out sounds*

The Fab Factor (aw au)

Green words: *Say the sounds. Say the word.*

cl<u>aws</u>   b<u>aw</u>l   f<u>au</u>lt   str<u>aw</u>   dr<u>aw</u>l

Say the syllables. Say the word.

a|<u>pp</u>l<u>au</u>se   <u>au</u>|di|en<u>ce</u>   M<u>au</u>r|een   n<u>augh</u>|ty   wi<u>th</u>|dr<u>aw</u>   t<u>au</u>nt|ing

Say the root word. Say the whole word.

y<u>aw</u>n → y<u>aw</u>ning

Red words: welc<u>ome</u>   <u>wh</u>at   c<u>all</u>   want   <u>sh</u>|ould   <u>who</u>

Challenge words: L<u>oui</u>s   t<u>augh</u>t   s<u>au</u>nters   gold   D<u>augh</u>ters   ind<u>ie</u>   s<u>au</u>cer   S<u>au</u>nders   b<u>ui</u>lding   Kermit   O'Bl<u>ear</u>y   <u>e͡ve</u>ning   introdu<u>ce</u>   Simon   T<u>ow</u>el   Sm<u>er</u>zy   he<u>ll</u>o   bro   private

---

Vocabulary check: **saunters** *walk in a slow, relaxed way*   **guffaw** *laugh*
taunting *to try and anger or provoke someone*